THE BEST
DOGS
EVER

SHIH TZUS
ARE THE
BEST!

Elaine Landau

LERNER PUBLICATIONS COMPANY · MINNEAPOLIS

For Barbara Stripling

Lerner Publications Company
A division of Lerner Publishing Group, Inc.
241 First Avenue North
Minneapolis, MN 55401 U.S.A.

Website address: www.lernerbooks.com

Library of Congress Cataloging-in-Publication Data

Landau, Elaine.
    Shih tzus are the best! / by Elaine Landau.
        p.   cm. — (The best dogs ever)
    Includes index.
    ISBN 978-1-58013-564-1 (lib. bdg. : alk. paper)
    1. Shih tzu—Juvenile literature. I. Title.
SF429.S64L36 2011
636.76—dc22   2009015267

Manufactured in the United States of America
1 — BP — 7/15/10

TABLE OF CONTENTS

CHAPTER ONE

A SUPER DOG

What do you look for in a dog? Would you like a pooch that is trusting and outgoing? What about a small dog with a big personality?

If these traits appeal to you, then you might like a **shih tzu!** These dogs have often been called little bundles of love.

A Pooch with Personality

Shih tzus make great companions. These cute canines will get along with your whole family. They even do well with other pets.

The shih tzu is also quite smart. Many shih tzu owners claim that their dogs can sense their moods.

DID YOU KNOW?

Shih tzu is a Chinese name. It's pronounced sheed-zoo.

The name *shih tzu* means "lion dog." Shih tzus got this name because some people thought they looked like little lions!

The photo on the right shows a statue of a Chinese lion. Do you think it looks like the shih tzu on the left?

Good Things Come in Small Packages

Shih tzus are sweet and petite. They are between 8 and 11 inches (20 and 28 centimeters) tall at the shoulder. That's a little shorter than a Barbie doll. They weigh between 9 and 16 pounds (4 to 7 kilograms). That's about as much as a large house cat.

Shih tzus have broad heads and short noses. Their eyes are large and round. These dogs are known for their wide-eyed, friendly look.

NAME THAT DOG!

Need a perfect name for your perfect pup? Maybe one of these will suit your new shih tzu.

Autumn
(for a golden shih tzu)

MUFFIN

Sultan

Tinker

Bubbles

Saucy

SNUGGLES

Petal

Tulip

DIZZY

Hair, Hair, Everywhere

Shih tzus also have very thick coats. Fur may be the first thing you notice when you look at these dogs! Their fur comes in many colors too. Some shih tzus are white with colored markings. Others are gold, black, or deep red.

A shih tzu with a short haircut looks very different from a long-haired dog!

SILENCE IS GOLDEN

Many small dogs bark a lot. And they often have high-pitched, squeaky barks. But shih tzus tend to be fairly quiet. These dogs are easy on the ears.

A Pint-Sized Joy

Shih tzus love being with their owners. It's hard to be lonely with these little dogs around. Their owners are sure they are the best dogs ever!

IN THE BEGINNING

Shih tzus have been around for about three thousand years. They first came from the Asian country of Tibet.

The Tibetan people thought shih tzus were holy. The dogs lived with monks, or religious leaders.

A Tibetan monk stands near a religious statue in 1917.

An Adored Dog

Monks sometimes gave shih tzus to Chinese emperors (powerful rulers) as gifts. In China, shih tzus were treated like royalty. The dogs had beds of the finest silk. They ate from the royal table.

This Chinese painting from around 750 shows a member of the royal court playing with her dog.

Shih tzus still get the royal treatment from their loving owners.

A Dog on the Move

For many years, shih tzus remained in China. But in the 1930s, these dogs were brought to England. They were later taken to other countries too.

This shih tzu arrived in England in 1954.

These three shih tzus traveled from Tibet to England in 1949.

Shih tzus became popular in the United States in the 1950s and 1960s. In 1969, the shih tzu was listed as a breed with the American Kennel Club (AKC).

Actress Zsa Zsa Gabor posed for this picture with her shih tzu around 1993.

THAT DOG IS A SWELL PAL

Shih tzus have always been great companions. That may be why these pretty pooches are sometimes used as therapy dogs. Therapy dogs are brought to hospitals or nursing homes. The patients there pet these comforting canines and feel better.

This shih tzu is a therapy dog. It helps people to feel less worried and alone.

The Joy of Owning a Toy

The AKC groups dogs by breed. Some of the AKC's groups are the sporting group, the herding group, and the working group. Shih tzus are in the toy group. Dogs in the toy group are all very small.

The komondor is part of the working group.

The English springer spaniel is part of the sporting group.

The collie is part of the herding group.

HALLMARK JOLEI SURFER GIRL

Most shih tzus are beloved house pets. But a few are also famous show dogs. A dog named Hallmark Jolei Surfer Girl *(right)* is one of these.

Known as Gidget at home, Surfer Girl came out a winner at the Westminster Kennel Club Dog Show. She took home the Best of Breed award on February 12, 2008.

Surfer Girl was picked out of fifteen other champion shih tzus. And the little dog was just twenty-one months old at the time!

These days, quite a few Americans own shih tzus. It's hard not to fall for these canine cuties. They are among the nation's ten most popular dog breeds.

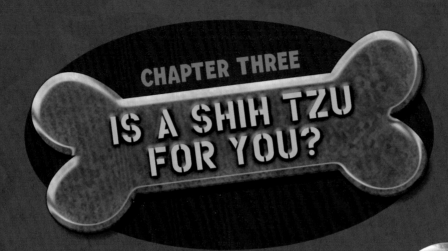

CHAPTER THREE

IS A SHIH TZU FOR YOU?

Shih tzus are both great looking and fun. That makes them the perfect dog for everyone— right? Not quite.

No breed is right for everyone. Here are a few things to think about before you bring a shih tzu home.

Not an Exercise Hound

Do you jog for hours? Can you hike for miles? Do you want to do this with your dog? Then don't get a shih tzu.

The shih tzu is a small dog with short legs. It will enjoy playing and going for walks. Just don't expect it to have endless energy and strength.

Not a Loner

The shih tzu is a people dog.
It does not like being alone
for long.

Are you busy most days after school? Are you out of the house a lot on weekends? While you are at school, will someone be at home with the dog?

A lonely shih tzu is an unhappy pooch. If you don't have much time for your dog, a shih tzu is not for you.

Shih tzus who are left alone a lot may get into trouble.

NOT A GREAT WATCHDOG

If you need a watchdog, don't get a shih tzu. It's just too sweet and friendly. It is more likely to greet a robber than attack one.

Groom Me, Please

A shih tzu needs lots of grooming. Are you willing to brush and comb your dog's coat every day?

Regular baths will keep your shih tzu's fur clean and soft.

Most shih tzu owners also take their dogs to professional groomers. The groomer bathes the dog, cuts its hair, and clips its nails. Groomers can be costly. Be sure your family can afford this before you get a shih tzu.

Even if the groomer gives your shih tzu a short haircut, it will still take lots of work to care for your dog's fur. Regular brushing is very important.

Remember to Be Gentle

A shih tzu is a sturdy little dog, but it isn't made of iron.
These dogs can be hurt during rough play. You'll have
to be gentle with your dog. The same goes for your
younger brothers and sisters.

PICKING OUT THAT SPECIAL DOG

Before buying a shih tzu, check out several different dogs of this breed. Do some of the dogs seem more playful than others? Do any of them seem very fearful? Seeing different dogs will help you pick the best one for you.

Now you know more about the shih tzu. Do you still think it's the right dog for you? If so, you've picked a terrific new friend.

If you're choosing between shih tzu puppies, spend some time getting to know their personalities.

CHAPTER FOUR

THE BEST DAY EVER

What was the best day of your life? Some shih tzu owners think it was the day they got their dog. That can be a super time for you too.

But before you bring your new pet home, you'll need a few supplies. Make sure you have the things you need to care for your four-footed friend.

Not sure what you'll need to welcome Fido to your family? This basic list is a great place to start:

- collar
- leash
- tags (for identification)
- dog food
- food and water bowls
- crates (one for when your pet travels by car and one for it to rest in at home)
- treats (to be used in training)
- toys

You might want to pick up a dog bed for your new friend too.

Has Your Dog Seen a Vet Yet?

You'll also want to take your dog to a veterinarian right away. A veterinarian, or vet, is a doctor who treats animals. The vet will check your dog's health. The vet will also give your shih tzu the shots it needs.

You'll be seeing the vet again. Soon your dog will need more shots. And you should take your dog to the vet if it gets sick.

LET'S PLAY

Have fun with your shih tzu. Roll a small squeaky ball across the floor. Let your shih tzu go for it!

Your shih tzu will also enjoy chasing soap bubbles. You can get tearless bubbles for dogs at many pet stores. These bubbles will not sting your dog's eyes.

Feeding Time!

Only feed your shih tzu dog food. Ask your vet which food would be best for your dog.

Don't be tempted to give your dog table scraps. A good diet will keep your dog lean and healthy. Also always leave out a bowl of cool water. Water is as important as food for your dog.

Dog treats make great rewards for your shih tzu when you're training it.

Playing with Your Pooch

Make your shih tzu feel loved. Take it on family outings. Invite your dog to your birthday party. Take it to a dog park too.

Your shih tzu will brighten your days. In return, give your dog the love and care it needs. Be good to your shih tzu, and the two of you will be the best of friends.

A LONG FRIENDSHIP

Did you know that small dogs tend to live longer than large ones? A shih tzu can often live from fifteen to eighteen years. Good food and medical care are important for a long, healthful life.

GLOSSARY

American Kennel Club (AKC): an organization that groups dogs by breed. The AKC also defines the characteristics of different breeds.

breed: a particular type of dog. Dogs of the same breed have the same body shape and general features.

canine: a dog, or having to do with dogs

coat: a dog's fur

diet: the food your dog eats

dog park: a special park where dogs can run and play off the leash

groom: to clean, brush, and trim a dog's coat

petite: very small

therapy dog: a dog brought to nursing homes or hospitals to comfort patients

toy group: a group of different types of dogs that are all small in size

veterinarian: a doctor who treats animals. Veterinarians are called vets for short.

FOR MORE INFORMATION

Books

Brecke, Nicole, and Patricia M. Stockland. *Dogs You Can Draw*. Minneapolis: Millbrook Press, 2010. In this book especially for dog lovers, Brecke and Stockland show how to draw many different types of dogs.

Gray, Susan H. *Shih Tzus*. Chanhassen, MN: Child's World, 2007. Learn what it's like to have a shih tzu in this fun text.

Hanson, Anders. *Shaggy Shih Tzus*. Edina, MN: Abdo, 2009. Hanson introduces interesting facts about shih tzus and provides a useful checklist to help readers choose the right dog for them.

Landau, Elaine. *Your Pet Dog*. Rev. ed. New York: Children's Press, 2007. This book is a good guide for young people on choosing and caring for a dog.

Simon, Seymour. *Dogs*. New York: HarperCollins, 2009. Find out more about dog intelligence and other characteristics in this interesting text.

Websites

American Kennel Club
http://www.akc.org
Visit this website to find a complete listing of AKC-registered dog breeds, including the shih tzu. The site also features fun printable activities for kids.

ASPCA Animaland
http://www2.aspca.org/site/PageServer?pagename=kids_pc_home
Check out this page for helpful hints on caring for a dog and other pets.

Index

Photo Acknowledgments

The images in this book are used with the permission of: © Larry Reynolds/dogpix.com, pp. 4, 8 (bottom), 23 (top); © Tanya Constantine/Photodisc/Getty Images, p. 5 (top), 9, 15 (bottom); © Glowimages/Getty Images, p. 5 (bottom right); © Pink Sun Media/Alamy, p. 5 (bottom left); © Klein J.-L. & Hubert M.-L./Peter Arnold, Inc., p. 6 (top); © Eric Isselée /StockphotoPro.com, p. 6 (bottom); Daniel Valla FRPS/Alamy, p. 7; © Doable/A. collection/Getty Images, p. 8 (top); © Historical Picture Archive/CORBIS, p. 10; © Bildarchiv Preussischer Kulturbesitz/Art Resource, NY, p. 11 (top); © tbkmedia.de/Alamy, p. 11 (bottom); © Mary Evans Picture Library/The Image Works, p. 12 (both); © Norman Parkinson Limited/CORBIS, p. 13 (top); © Anne Chadwick Williams/(Sacramento Bee)/ZUMA Press, p. 13 (bottom); © Isselee/Dreamstime.com, p. 14 (springer spaniel); © Dorling Kindersley/Getty Images, p. 14 (komandor); © Eric Isselee/Shutterstock Images, p. 14 (collie); REUTERS/Lucas Jackson, p. 15 (top); © Ken Hurst/Shutterstock Images, p. 16; © Charlie Newton/(The San Diego Union Tribune)/ZUMA Press, p. 17 (top); © Hermes Images/Photolibrary, p. 17 (bottom); © Angie Knost/Alamy, p. 18; © Top-Pet-Pics/Alamy, p. 19 (top); © Geri Lavrov/SuperStock, pp. 19 (bottom), 22, 25, 27 (top); © O.DIGOIT/Alamy , p. 20 (top); © Purestock/Getty Images, p. 20 (bottom); © Gareth Brown/CORBIS, p. 21 (top); © Yellow Dog Productions/Riser/Getty Images, p. 21 (bottom); © iStockphoto.com/Ken Hurst, p. 23 (bottom); © Jupiterimages/Brand X Pictures/Getty Images, p. 24; © Tooties/Dreamstime.com, p. 26 (top); © Uturnpix/Dreamstime.com, p. 26 (second from top); istockphoto.com/Orix3, p. 26 (second from bottom); WILDLIFE/Peter Arnold Inc., p. 26 (bottom); Linda Kennedy/Alamy, p. 27 (bottom); © AnnieAnnie/Dreamstime.com, p. 28 (top); © Mathew Benoit/ Shutterstock Images, p. 28 (bottom); © Tristan Hawke/PhotoStockFile/Alamy, p. 29.

Front cover: © Eric Isselee/Shutterstock Images.
Back cover: © Joanna Totolici/Workbook Stock/Getty Images.